The Autobiography of Sir William Topaz McGonagall

William McGonagall

The Autobiography

of

Sir William Topaz McGonagall

Poet and Tragedian

Knight of the White Elephant, Burmah

My Dear Readers of this autobiography, which I am the author of, I beg leave to inform you that I was born in Edinburgh. My parents were born in Ireland, and my father was a handloom weaver, and he learned me the handloom weaving while in Dundee, and I followed it for many years, until it began to fail owing to machinery doing the weaving instead of the handloom. So much so as I couldn't make a living from it. But I may say Dame Fortune has been very kind to me by endowing me with the genius of poetry. I remember how I felt when I received the spirit of poetry. It was in the year of 1877, and in the month of June, when trees and flowers were in full bloom. Well, it being the holiday week in Dundee, I was sitting in my back room in Paton's Lane, Dundee, lamenting to myself because I couldn't get to the Highlands on holiday to see the beautiful scenery, when all of a sudden my body got inflamed, and instantly I was seized with a strong desire to write poetry, so strong, in fact, that in imagination I thought I heard a voice crying in my ears-

"WRITE! WRITE"

I wondered what could be the matter with me, and I began to walk backwards and forwards in a great fit of excitement, saying to myself— "I know nothing about poetry." But still the voice kept ringing in my ears - "Write, write," until at last, being overcome with a desire to write poetry, I found paper, pen, and ink, and in a state of frenzy, sat me down to think what would be my first subject for a, poem. All at once I thought of the late Rev. George Gilfillan, and composed a poem of four stanzas in his praise as a preacher, and orator, and poet. Then I sent it to the "Weekly News" for publication, not sending my name with it, only my initials - W. McG., Dundee. It was published, along with a short comment by the editor in its praise, as follows:— " W. McG., Dundee, has sent us a poem in praise of the Rev. George Gilfillan, and he sung his praises truly and well, but he modestly seeks to hide his light under a bushel" so when I read the poem in the "Weekly News" I was highly pleased no doubt to see such a favourable comment regarding it. Then my next poem, or second, was the "Railway Bridge of the Silvery

Tay", which caused a great sensation in Dundee and far away. In fact, gentle readers, it was the only poem that made me famous universally. The reading of the poem abroad caused the Emperor of Brazil to leave his home far away incognito and view the bridge as he passed along *en route* to Inverness. But, my dear readers, the Tay Bridge poem is out of print, and I do not intend to publish it again, owing to the fall of the bridge in the year of 1879, which will be remembered for a very long time.

I may also state in this short autobiography of mine that my parents are dead some years ago — I don't remember how many, but they are buried in the Eastern Necropolis, Dundee, and I may say they were always good to me.

And now concerning something more attractive, my dear readers, I must inform ye that as early as ten years of age I was very fond of reading Shakespeare's Penny Plays (Vicker's edition), and from them I received great knowledge regarding the histrionic art. The plays or tragedies I studied most were Macbeth, Hamlet, Richard III, and Othello, the Moor of Venice, and these four characters I have impersonated in my time. During my stay in Dundee my

FIRST APPEARANCE ON THE STAGE

was in the character of Macbeth in Mr Giles' Penny Theatre, Lindsay Street, Dundee, to an overflowing end crowded audience, and I received unbounded applause. I was called before the curtain several times during the performance, and I remember the actors of the company felt very jealous owing to me getting the general applause, and several were as bold as tell me so; and when it came to the combat scene betwixt me and Macduff the actor who was playing Macduff against my Macbeth tried to spoil me in the combat by telling me to cut it short, so as the audience, in his opinion, would say it was a poor combat, but I was too cute for him, guessing his motive for it. I continued the combat until he were fairly exhausted, and until there was one old gentleman in the audience cried out, "Well done, McGonagall! Walk into him! " And so I did until he was in a great rage, and stamped his foot, and cried out, "Fool! Why don't you fall ?" And when I did fall the cry was "McGonagall! McGonagall! Bring him out! Bring him out! " until I had to come before the curtain and receive an ovation from the audience. Such was the case in my second appearance, under the management of Forrest Knowles in the Grocers' Hall, Castle Street, Dundee. The characters I appeared in under his management were Macbeth, Richard III, and Hamlet. These three characters I performed to crowded and delighted audiences. I remember Mr Knowles told me in the dressing-room that I looked the character so well in the dress that I should wear it, and not throw it off, but I told him it was too great a joke to say so. I also remember on that night there were several gentlemen in the audience who were from Edinburgh, and they came to my dressing-room to congratulate me on my great success, and shook hands with me, telling me that few professionals could do it so well; but perhaps they were only flattering me. If so, I will say with the poet, John Dryden —

> Flattery, like ice, our footing does betray,
> Who can tread sure on the smooth slippery way?

Pleased with the fancy, we glide swiftly on,
And see the dangers which we cannot shun.

My dear readers, the next strange adventure in my life was my

JOURNEY TO BALMORAL

to see the bonnie Highland floral and Her Gracious Majesty the
Queen, who was living in Balmoral Castle, near by the River Dee.
Well, I left Dundee in the month of June, 1878. I remember it was a
beautiful sunshiny day, which made my heart feel light and gay, and
I tramped to Alyth that day, and of course I felt very tired end
footsore owing to the intense heat. The first thing I thought about
was to secure lodgings for the night, which I secured very easily
without any trouble, and then I went and bought some groceries for
my supper and breakfast, such as tea, sugar, butter, and bread. Then
I prepared my supper, and ate heartily, for I had not tasted food of
any kind since I had left Dundee, and the distance I had travelled
was fifteen miles, and with the fresh air I had inhaled by the way it
gave me a keen appetite, and caused me to relish my supper, and
feel content. Then the landlady of the house, being a kind-hearted
woman, gave me some hot water to wash my feet, as she thought it

4

would make my feet feel more comfortable, and cause me to sleep more sound. And after I had gone to bed I slept as sound as if I'd been dead, and arose in the morning quite refreshed and vigorous after the sound sleep I had got. Then I washed my hands and face, and prepared my breakfast, and made myself ready for the road again, with some biscuits in my pocket and a pennyworth of cheese. I left, Alyth about ten o'clock in the morning, and crossed over a dreary moor, stunted and barren in its aspect, which was a few miles in length — I know not how many — but I remember there were only two houses to be met with all the way, which caused me to feel rather discontented indeed. The melancholy screams of the peesweeps overhead were rather discordant sounds ringing in my ears, and, worst of all, the rain began to fall heavily, and in a short time I felt wet to the skin; and the lightning began to flash and the thunder to roar. Yet I trudged on manfully not the least daunted, for I remembered of saying to my friends in Dundee I would pass through fire and water rather than turn tail, and make my purpose good, as I had resolved to see Her Majesty at Balmoral. I remember by the roadside there was a big rock, and behind it I took shelter from the rain a few moments, and partook of my bread and cheese, while the rain kept pouring down in torrents. After I bed taken my luncheon I rose to my feet, determined to push on in spits of rain and thunder, which made me wonder, because by this time I was about to enter

On the Spittal of Glenshee,
Which is most dismal for to see,
With its bleak and rugged mountains,
And clear, crystal, spouting fountains
With their misty foam;
And thousands of sheep there together doth roam,
Browsing on the barren pasture most gloomy to see.
Stunted in heather, and scarcely a tree,
Which is enough to make the traveller weep,
The loneliness thereof and the bleating of the sheep.

However, I travelled on while the rain came pouring down copiously and I began to feel very tired, and longed for rest, for by this time I had travelled about thirteen miles, and the road on

THE SPITTAL OF GLENSHEE

I remember was very stony in some parts. I resolved to call at the first house I saw by the way and ask lodgings for the night. Well, the first home chanced to be a shepherd's, and I called at the door and gently knocked, and my knock was answered by the mistress of the house. When she saw me she asked me what I wanted, and I told her I wanted a night's lodging and how I was wet to the skin. Then she bade me come inside and sit down by the fireside and dry my claes, and tak' aff my shoon end warm my feet at the fire, and I did so. Then I told her I came from Dundee, and that I was going to Balmoral to see Her Majesty the Queen, end that I was a poet. When I said I was a poet her manner changed altogether and she asked me if I would take some porridge if she made some, and I said I would and feel very thankful for them. So in a short time the porridge were made, and as quickly partaken, and in a short time the shepherd came in with his two collie dogs, and the mistress told him I was a traveller from Dundee and a poet. When he heard I was a poet he asked me my name, and I told him I was McGonagall, the poet. He seemed o'erjoyed when be heard me say so, and told me I was welcome as a lodger for the night, and to make myself at home, and that he had heard often about me. I chanced to have a few copies of a twopence edition of poems with me from Dundee and I gave him a copy, and he seemed to be highly pleased with reading the poems during the evening, especially the one about the late George Gilfillan, and for the benefit of my readers I will insert it as follows. I may also state this is the first poem I composed, when I received the gift of poetry, which appeared in the "Weekly News" : —

LINES IN PRAISE OF THE REV. GEORGE GILFILLAN

All hail to the Rev. George Gilfillan, of Dundee,
He is the greatest preacher I did ever hear or see.
He preaches in a plain, straightforward way,
The people flock to hear him night and day,
And hundreds from his church doors are often turned away,
Because he is the greatest preacher of the present day.
The first time I heard him speak 'twas in the Kinnaird Hall,
Lecturing on the Garabaldi movement as loud as he could bawl.
He is a charitable gentlemen to the poor while in distress,
And for his kindness unto them the Lord will surely bless.
My blessing on his noble form and on his lofty head.
May all good angels guard him while living and hereafter when
    dead.

Well, my dear readers, after the shepherd and me had a social confab together concerning Gilfillan end poetry for some time his wife came in, and she said, "Guidman, I've been out making a bed for you in the barn. But maybe ye'll be feared tae sleep in the barn." But I said, "Oh, no, my good woman, not in the least." So she told her husband to show me the way to the barn, and he said, "Oh, yes, I'll do that, and feel, highly honoured in doing so." Accordingly he got a lantern and lighted it, and then said — "Come along with me, sir, and I'll show you where to sleep for the night." Then he led the way to the barn, and when he entered he showed me the bed, and I can assure you it was a bed suitable for either King or Queen.

> And the blankets and sheets
> Were white and clean,
> And most beautiful to be seen,
> And I'm sure would have pleased Lord Aberdeen.

Then the shepherd told me I could bar the barn door if I liked if I was afraid to sleep without it being barred, and I said I would bar the door, considering it much safer to do so. Then he bade me good-night, hoping I would sleep well and come in to breakfast in the morning.

A STRANGE DREAM

After the shepherd had bidden me good-night I barred the door, and went to bed, as I expected to sleep; but for a long time I couldn't — until at last I was in the arms of Morpheus, dreaming I was travelling betwixt a range of mountains, and seemingly to be very misty, especially the mountain tops. Then I thought I saw a carriage and four horses, and seemingly two drivers, and also a lady in the carriage, who I thought would be the Queen. Then the carriage vanished all of a sudden, and I thought I had arrived at Balmoral Castle, and in front of the Castle I saw a big Newfoundland dog, and he kept barking loudly and angry at me but I wasn't the least afraid of him, and as I advanced towards the front door of the Castle he sprang at me, and seized my right hand, and bit it severely, until it bled profusely. I seemed to feel it painful, and when I awoke, my dear readers, I was shaking with fear, and considered it to be a warning or a bad omen to me on my journey to Balmoral. But, said I to myself —

"Hence babbling dreams!
You threaten me in vain."

Then I tried hard to sleep, but couldn't. So the night stole tediously away, and morning came at last, peeping through the chinks of the barn door. So I arose, and donned my clothes, then went into the shepherd's house, but the shepherd wasn't in. He'd been away two hours ago, the mistress said, to look after the sheep on the rugged mountains. "But sit ye down, guidman," said she, "and I'll mak' some porridge for ye before ye tak' the road, for it's a dreary road to Balmoral. So I thanked her and husband for their kindness towards me, and telling her to give my best wishes to her husband bade her good-bye and left the shepherd's house for the Queen's Castle.

It was about ten o'clock in the morning when I left the shepherd's house at the Spittal of Glenshee on my journey to Balmoral. I expected to be there about three o'clock in the afternoon. Well, I travelled on courageously, and, when Balmoral Castle hove in sight, I saw the Union Jack unfurled to the breeze. Well, I arrived at the Castle just as the tower clock was chiming the hour of three. But my heart wasn't full of glee, because I had a presentiment that I wouldn't succeed. When I arrived at the lodge gate, I knocked loudly at the door of the lodge, and it was answered by a big, burly-looking man, dressed in a suit of pilot cloth. He boldly asked me what I wanted and where I had come from. I told him I had travelled all the way from Dundee expecting to see Her Majesty, and to be permitted to give an entertainment before her in the Castle from my own works and from the works of Shakespeare. Further, I informed him that I was the Poet McGonagall, and how I had been patronised by Her Majesty. I showed him Her Majesty's letter of patronage, which he read, and said it was a forgery. I said, if he thought so, he could have me arrested. He said this thinking to frighten me, but, when he saw he couldn't, he asked me if I would give him a recital in front of the Lodge as a specimen of my abilities. "No, sir," I said; "nothing so low in my line of business. I am

NOT A STROLLING MOUNTEBANK

that would do the like in the open air for a few coppers. Take me into one of the rooms in the Lodge, and pay me for it, and I will give you a recital, and upon no consideration will I consent to do it in the open air."

Just at that time there was a young lady concealed behind the Lodge door hearkening all the time unknown to me. The man said, "Will you not oblige the young lady here?" And when I saw the lady I said, "No, sir. Nor if Her Majesty would request me to do it in the open air, I wouldn't yield to her request." Then he said, "So I see, but I must tell you that nobody can see Her Majesty without an introductory letter from some nobleman to certify that they are safe to be ushered into Her Majesty's presence, and remember, if ever you come here again, you are liable to be arrested." So I bade him good-bye, and came away without dismay, and crossed o'er a little iron bridge there which spans the River Dee, which is magnificent to see. I went in quest of lodgings for the night, and, as I looked towards the west, I saw a farmhouse to the right of me, about half a mile from the highway. To it I went straightaway, and knocked at the door gently, and a voice from within cried softly, "Come in." When I entered an old man and woman were sitting by the fireside, and the man bade me sit down. I said I was very thankful for the seat, because I was tired and footsore, and required lodging for the night, and that I had been at Balmoral Castle expecting to see Her Majesty, and had been denied the liberty of seeing her by the constable at the Lodge gate. When I told him I had travelled all the way on foot from Dundee, he told me very feelingly he would allow me to stay with him for two or three days, and I could go to the roadside, where Her Majesty passed almost every day, and he was sure she would speak to me, as she always spoke to the gipsies and gave them money. The old woman, who was sitting in the corner at her tea, said, "By, and mind ya, guidman, it's no silver she gives them, it's gold. I'm sure Her Majesty's a richt guid lady. Mind ye, this is the Queen's bread I'm eating. Guidman, the mair, I canna see you. I'm blind, born blind, and I maun tell ye, as you're a poet, as I heard ye say, the Queen alloos a' the auld wimmen in the district here a loaf of bread, tea, and sugar, and a' the cold meat that's no used at the Castle, and, mind ye, ilka ane o' them gets an equal share." I said it was very kind of Her Majesty to do so, and she said, "That's no' a', guidman. She aye finds wark for idle men when she comes here— wark that's no needed, no' for hersel, athegether, but just to help needy folk, and I'm sure if you see her she will help you." So I thanked her for the information I had got, and then was conducted to my bed in the barn— a very good one— after I had got a good supper of porridge and milk. Then I went to bed,

NOT TO SLEEP, BUT TO THINK

of the treatment I had met with from the constable at the lodge of Balmoral Castle. I may state also that I showed the constable at the lodge a copy of my poems — twopence edition — I had with me, and he asked me the price of it, and I said, "Twopence, please." Then he chanced to notice on the front of it, "Poet to Her Majesty," and he got into a rage and said, "You're not poet to Her Majesty." Then I said, "You cannot deny that I am patronised by Her Majesty." Then he said, "Ah, but you must know Lord Tennyson is the real poet to Her Majesty. However, I'll buy this copy of your poems." But, as I said before, when I went to bed it was to think, not to sleep, and I thought in particular what the constable told me— if ever I chanced to come the way again I would be arrested, and the thought thereof caused an undefinable fear to creep all over my body. I actually shook with fear, which I considered to be a warning not to attempt the like again. So I resolved that in the morning I would go home again the may I came. All night through I tossed and turned from one side to another, thinking to sleep, but to court it was all in vain, and as soon as daylight dawned I arose and made ready to take the road. Then I went to the door of the farmhouse and knocked, and it was answered by the farmer, and he said, "'Odsake, guidman, hoo have ye risen sae early? It's no' five o'clock yet. Gae awa' back to your bed and sleep twa or three hours yet, and ye will hae plenty o' time after that tae gang tae the roadside to see Her Majesty." But I told him I had given up all thought of it, that I was afraid the constable at the lodge would be on the lookout for me, and if he saw me loitering about the roadside he would arrest me and swear falsely against me. Then he said, " Guidman, perhaps it's the safest way no' to gang, but, however, you'll need some breakfast afore ye tak' the road, sae come in by and sit doon there." Then he asked me if I could sup brose, and I said I could, and be thankful for the like. Then he cried, " Hi! lassie, come here and bile the kettle quick and mak' some brose for this guidman before he gangs awa'." Then the lassie came ben. She might have been about sixteen or seventeen years old, and in a short time she had the kettle boiling, and prepared for me a cog of brose and milk, which I supped greedily and cheerfully, owing no doubt to the pure Highland air I had inhaled, which gave me a keen appetite. Then the farmer came ben and bade me good-bye, and told me to be sure and call again if ever I came the way, and how I would be sure to get a night's lodging or two or three if I liked to stay. So I bade him good-bye and the lassie and the old blind woman, thanking them for their kindness towards me. But the farmer said to the lassie," Mak' up a piece bread and cheese for him for fear he'll no' get muckle meat on the Spittal o' Glenshee." So when I got the piece of bread and cheese again I bade them good-bye, and took the road for Glenshee, bound for Dundee, while the sun shone out bright and clear, which did my spirits cheer. After I had travelled about six miles, my feet got very hot, and in a very short time both were severely blistered. So I sat me down to rest me for a while, and while I rested I ate of my piece bread and cheese, which, I'm sure, did me please, and gave me fresh strength and enabled me to resume my travel again. I travelled on another six miles until I arrived at a lodging-house by the roadside, called

THE MILLER'S LODGING-HOUSE

because he had been a meal miller at one time. There I got a bed for the night, and paid threepence for it, and I can assure ye it was a very comfortable one; and the mistress of the house made some porridge for me by my own request, and gave me some milk, for which she charged me twopence. When I had taken my porridge, she gave me some hot water in a little tub to wash my feet, because they were blistered, and felt very sore. And when my feet were washed I went to my bed, and in a short time I was sound asleep. About eight o'clock the next morning I awoke quite refreshed, because I had slept well during the night, owing to the goodness of the bed and me being so much fatigued with travelling. Then I chanced to have a little tea and sugar in my pocket that I had bought in Alyth, so I asked the landlady if she could give me a teapot, as I had some tea with me in my pocket, and I would infuse it for my breakfast, as I hadn't got much tea since I had left Dundee. So she gave me a teapot, and I infused the tea, and drank it cheerfully, end ate the remainder of my cheese and bread. I remember it was a lovely sunshiny morning when I bade my host and hostess good-bye, and left, resolved to travel to Blairgowrie, and lodge there for the night. So I travelled on the best way I could. My feet felt very sore, but

> As I chanced to see trouts louping in the River o' Glenshee,
> It helped to fill my heart with glee,
> And to anglers I would say without any doubt
> There's plenty of trouts there for pulling out.

When I saw them louping and heard the birds singing o'erhead it really seemed to give me pleasure, and to feel more contented than I would have been otherwise. At Blairgowrie I arrived about seven o'clock at night, and went in quest of a lodging-house, and found one easy enough, and for my bed I paid fourpence in advance. And when I had secured my bed I went out to try to sell a few copies of my poems I had with me from Dundee the twopence edition, and I managed to sell half a dozen of copies with a great struggle. However, I was very thankful, because it would tide me over until I would arrive in Dundee. So with the shilling I had earned from my poems I bought some grocery goods, and prepared my supper — tea, of course, and bread and butter. Then I had my feet washed, and went to bed, and slept as sound as if I'd been dead. In the morning I arose about seven o'clock, and prepared my breakfast— tea again, and breed and butter. Then after my breakfast I washed my hands and face, end started for Dundee at a rapid pace, and thought it no disgrace. Still the weather kept good, and the sun shone bright and clear, which did my spirits cheer, and weary and footsore I trudged along, singing a verse of a hymn, not a song, as follows :—

> Our poverty and trials here
> Will only make us richer there,
> When we arrive at home, &c., &c.

When at the ten milestone from Dundee I sat down and rested for a while, and partook of a piece bread and butter. I toiled on manfully, and arrived in Dundee about eight o'clock, unexpectedly to my friends and acquaintances. So this, my dear friends, ends my famous journey to Balmoral. Next morning I had a newspaper reporter wanting the particulars regarding my journey to Balmoral, and in my simplicity of heart I gave him all the information regarding it, and when it was published in the papers it

CAUSED A GREAT SENSATION

In fact, it was the only thing that made me famous — it and the Tay Bridge poem. I was only one week in Dundee after coming from Balmoral when I sent a twopence edition of my poems to the late Rev. George Gilfillan, who was on a holiday tour at Stonehaven at the time for the good of his health. He immediately sent me a reply, as follows:—

The Autobiography of Sir William Topaz McGonagall

Stonehaven, June, 1878.

Dear Sir,— I thank you for your poems, especially the kind lines addressed to myself. I have read of your famous journey to Balmoral, for which I hope you are none the worse. I am here on holiday, but return in a few days.— Believe me, yours truly,

GEORGE GILFILLAN.

Well, the next stirring event in my life which I consider worth narrating happened this way. Being out one day at the little village of Fowlis, about six miles from Dundee, and being in rather poor circumstances, I thought of trying to get a schoolroom to give an entertainment. But when I applied for the schoolroom I met with a refusal Therefore, not to be beat, I resolved to try to get the smithy, and was fortunate in getting it.

Then I went all over the village, or amongst the people, inviting them to my entertainment, chiefly from my own works and from Shakespeare. The prices were to be— Adults 2d., boys and girls 1d., and the performance was to commence at eight o'clock precisely. Well, when I had made it known amongst the villagers, some of them promised to come— chiefly ploughmen and some of the scholars. To while away the time, I called at the smith's house. The family had just sat down to supper, and the smith bade me draw in a chair to the table and take some supper, which consisted of tea end plenty of oaten cakes and loaf bread; also ham, cheese, and butter. So of course I drew in by my chair to the table, and fared very sumptuously, because I had got no refreshment since the morning before leaving Dundee. After supper, the smith said he would gang doon to the smithy wi' me, and gie it a bit redd up and get the lamp lighted.

THE SMITHY ENTERTAINMENT

In a short time a few ploughmen came, and of course I was at the door to take the money, and they asked me the charge of admission, and I said— "Twopence, please." Then a few more people came — old and young — and they all seemed to be quite happy in expectation of the coming entertainment. When it was near eight o'clock the smith told me I would need to make ready to begin, so I told him to take the money at the door, and I would begin. He said he would do that cheerfully, and he took his stand at the door, and I addressed the audience as follows:— "Ladies and gentlemen, with your permission, I will now make a beginning by reciting my famous poem, 'Bruce at Bannockburn.'" Before it was half finished I received great applause; and when finished they were all delighted. Then followed "The Battle of Tel-El-Kebir" and a scene from "Macbeth"; also "The Rattling Boy from Dublin," which concluded the evening's entertainment. The proceeds taken at the door amounted to 4s. 9d., and of course I was well pleased with what I had realised, because it is a very poor locality in that part of the country. Well, I thanked the audience for their patronage; also the smith for allowing me the use of his smithy, and, bidding him good-night, I came away resolving to travel home again straightway. Well, as I drew near to Fowlis Schoolroom I heard the pattering of feet behind me and the sound of men's voices. So I was instantly seized with an indefinable fear, and I grasped my stick firmly in my right hand, and stood stock still, resolved to wait until the party behind would come up, and stood right in front of me, and neither of us spoke, when the centre man of the three whispered something to the two men that was with him, and then he threw out both arms, with the intention, no doubt, as I thought, of pulling my hat down over my eyes; but no sooner were his arms thrown out than my good oaken cudgel came across his body with full force.

My Dear Friends,— I cannot describe to you my feelings at that moment. The cold sweat started to my forehead, but I was resolved to strike out in self-defence. Well, when I brought my good oaken cudgel over the ringleader's body he sprang back, and whispered to his companions, and they were forced to retire. As they were going the same road home as I was going, I thought it advisable not to go, so I took a back road, which leads up to the village of Birkhill, five miles from Dundee, and when I arrived at the village it was past eleven o'clock at night. I went direct to the constable's house and rapped at the door, and it was answered by himself demanding who was there. I said, "A friend," so he opened the door, and he said— "Oh, it's you, Mr McGonagall. Come in. Well, sir, what do you want at this late hour?" "Well, sir," I said, "I've been down to-night giving an entertainment in the Smithy of Fowlis, and I've been attacked near to the Schoolroom of Fowlis by three men that followed me. One of the three, the centre one. threw out both of his arms, with the intention, no doubt, of pulling my hat down over my eyes; but this stick, sir, of mine, went whack against his body, which made him and his companions retire from the field. And now, as I am rather afraid to pass through Lord Duncan's woods, which are rather dreary and lonely, and the night being so dark, I want you sir, to escort me through the woods." Then he said he couldn't do that, looking to the lateness of the night, but, said he, "Just you go on, and if anyone offers to molest you, just shout as loud as you can, and I'll come to you." "But, my dear sir," I said, "three men could have me murdered before you could save me." "Well," he said, " I'll stand at the door for a little to see if anyone molests you, and I'll bid you good-night, Mr McGonagall, and safe home." I remember while passing through Lord Duncan's woods I recited to myself—

Yet though I walk through death's dark vale,
Yet will I fear none ill,
For Thou art with me, and Thy rod
And staff me comfort still.

Well, thank God, my dear friends, I arrived safe home to Dundee shortly after twelve o'clock, and my family were very glad to see me safe home again, asking me why I had been so late in coming home. When I told them what I had been doing, giving an entertainment in the Smithy of Fowlis, and had been set upon by three men, they were astonished to hear it, end said that I should thank God that had saved me from being murdered. However, the four shillings and ninepence I fetched home with me — that I had gained from my entertainment — I gave all to my wife, and she was very thankful to get it, became the wolf was at the door, and it had come very opportune. Well, after I had warmed myself at the fire, and taken a cup of tea, and bread and butter, I went to bed, but didn't sleep very sound. I suppose that was owing to the three men that attacked me in the home-coming. Well, my dear readers, the next stirring event that I will relate is

MY TRIP TO AMERICA

In my remembrance, that is about fourteen years ago, and on the 9th of March I left Dundee. But before I left it I went amongst all my best friends and bade them good-bye, but one particular good friend I must mention, the late Mr Alexander C. Lamb, proprietor of the Temperance Hotel, Dundee. Well, when I called to bid him good-bye, and after we had shaken hands warmly, he asked me if any of my pretended friends had promised to take me home again from America if I failed in my enterprise. So I told him not one amongst them had promised. "Well," says he, "write to me and I will fetch you home."

Then on the next day after bidding good-bye to my friends and relations in Dundee, I left Dundee with the train bound for Glasgow, and arrived safe about four o'clock in the afternoon. When I arrived I went to a good temperance hotel, near to the

Broomielaw Bridge, and secured lodgings for the night, and before going to bed I prepared my supper— tea, of course, and bread and butter — and made a good meal of it. Then I went to bed, but I didn't sleep very sound, because my mind was too much absorbed regarding the perilous adventure I was about to undertake. Well, at an early hour the next morning I got up and washed myself and prepared my breakfast, and made ready to embark on board the good steamship "Circassia," bound for the city of New York. When I went on board all was confusion, and there was a continuous babel of voices amongst the passengers, each one running hither and thither in search of a berth. And I can assure ye, my friends, it was with a great deal of trouble I secured a berth, because there were so many passengers on board. Well, when all the passengers had got their berths secured for the voyage, and the anchor had been weighed, and the sails hoisted, the big steamer left the Clyde with upwards of 500 souls, bound for New York. Some of them were crying, and some were singing, and some were dancing to the stirring strains of the pibroch. Such is life I say, throughout the world every day, and it was on the 10th of March we sailed away bound for America. As the stout steamer entered the waters of the Atlantic Ocean some snow began to fall, and a piercing gale of wind sprang up, but the snow soon ceased, and the wind ceased also, and the vessel sped on rapidly through the beautiful blue sea, while the cooks on board were preparing the passengers' tea. Yes, my dear readers, that's the supper the passengers get every night— plenty of bread, butter, and tea; and coffee, bread, and butter for breakfast; and for dinner, broth or soup and bread and beef. This is the fare in general going and coming. Well, when a week at sea all of a sudden the vessel began to roll, and the sea got into a billowy swell. The vessel began to heave fearfully, and the big waves began to lash her sides and sweep across her deck, so that all the boxes and chests on deck and below had to be firmly secured to prevent them from getting tossed about, and to prevent them from making a roaring sound like thunder. Many of the passengers felt seasick, and were vomiting, but I didn't feel sick at all. Well, the next day was a beautiful sunny day, and all the passengers felt gay, and after tea was over it was proposed amongst a few of them to get up

A CONCERT ON BOARD

that night. I was invited by a few gentlemen, and selected as one of the performers for the evening, and was told to dress in Highland costume, and that I would receive a collection for the recitations I gave them. The concert was to begin at eight o'clock. Well, I consented to take part in the concert, and got a gentleman to dress me, and when dressed I went to the second cabin, where the concert was to be held, and when I entered the cabin saloon I received a hearty round of applause from the passengers gathered there. Among them were the chief steward of the vessel. He was elected as chairman for the evening, and addressed us as follows:— "Ladies and gentlemen,— I wish it to be understood that all collections of money taken on board this vessel at concerts go for the benefit of the Lifeboat Fund, and I also hope you will also enjoy yourselves in a decent way, and get through with the concert about ten o'clock, say. As Mr McGonagall, the great poet, is first on the programme, I will call on him to recite his own poem 'Bruce at Bannockburn.'"

So I leapt to my feet and commenced, and before I was right begun I received a storm of applause, but that was all I received for it. Well, when I came to the thrusts and cuts with my sword my voice was drowned with applause, and when I had finished I bade them all good-night, and retired immediately to my berth in the steerage, and undressed myself quickly, and went to bed, resolving in my mind not to dress again if I was requested on the home-coming voyage. Well, my friends, the vessel made the voyage to New York in twelve days— of course night included as well— and when she arrived at the jetty or harbour of New York some of the passengers, when they saw it, felt glad, and others felt sad, especially those that had but little money with them. As for myself, I had but eight shillings, which made me feel very downcast, because all the passengers are examined at Castle

Gardens by the officials there regarding the money they have with them, and other properties.

Well, when I came to the little gate where all the passengers are questioned regarding their trades and names before they are allowed to pass, and if they want their British money changed for American money, I saw at once how I could manage. So after the man had entered my name and trade in his book as a weaver, I took from my purse the eight shillings, and laid it down fearlessly, and said— "Change that! It is all I require in the meantime." So the man looked at me dubiously, but I got passed without any more trouble after receiving the American money, Then I passed on quickly until I saw a car passing along the way I was going. So I got into the car, and I asked the carman where was Forty-Nine Street. He said he was just going along that way, and he would let me off the car when he came to it. So he did, honestly. Then I went to an old acquaintance of mine while in Dundee, and rang the door bell, and it was answered by my friend. When he saw me he stood aghast in amazement, but he bade me come in, and when I entered the house his wife bade me sit down, and sit near to the fire, for nae doubt I would feel cold after being on the sea sae lang. So the mistress said I'll mak' ye a cup o' tea, for ye'll be hungry, nae doubt, and I said I was so. Tea was prepared immediately, and my friend and his wife sat down at the table together, and made a hearty meal, and seemingly they were very sociable until we had finished eating, and the table removed. Then my friend asked me why I had ventured to come to New York. So I told him it was in expectation of getting engagements in music halls in the city, and he said he was afraid I wouldn't succeed in getting an engagement. As he said it came to pass, for when I went three days after being in New York to look for engagements at the music halls I was told by all the managers I saw that they couldn't give me an engagement, because there was a combination on foot

AGAINST ALL BRITISH ARTISTS

and how I had come at a very bad time. When I couldn't get an engagement I thought I would try and sell some of my poems I had fetched with me from Dundee. Well, the first day I tried to sell them it was a complete failure for this reason— When they saw the Royal coat of arms on the top of the poems they got angry, and said, "To the deuce with that. We won't buy that here. You'll better go home again to Scotland." Well, of course, I felt a little angry, no doubt, and regretted very much that I had been so unlucky as to come to New York, and resolved in my mind to get home again as soon as possible. When I came back to my friend's house, or my lodging-house in New York, I told him how I had been treated when I offered my poems for sale, and he said to me, " I'll tell you what to do. You'll just cut off the Royal coat-of-arms, and then the people will buy them from you." And when he told me to do so I was astonished to hear him say so, and told him "No!" I said, "I decline to do so. I am not ashamed of the Royal coat-of-arms yet, and I think you ought to be ashamed for telling me so, but you may think as you like, I will still adhere to my colours wherever I go."

WEARYING FOR HOME

Well, after I had been three weeks in New York without earning a
cent I thought I would write home to Dundee to Mr Alexander C.
Lamb, proprietor of the Temperance Hotel, Dundee. Well, I
remember when writing to my dear friend, the late Mr Lamb, I told
him for God's sake to take me home from out of this second Babylon,
for I could get no one to help me, and when writing it the big tears
were rolling down my cheeks, and at the end of the letter I told him
to address it to the Anchor Line Steam Shipping Company's office, to
lie till called for. So, when the letter was finished I went out to the
Post Office and posted it. Well, to be brief, I remember the next day
was Sunday, and in the evening of the same day my friend invited
the most of his neighbours to his house, as there was going to be a
concert held amongst them, and, of course, I was invited to the
concert and expected to recite, of course. And after the neighbours
had been all seated and ready to begin my friend was elected by the
neighbours to occupy the chair for the evening, and he said, "Ladies
and gentlemen,— As we are all assembled here to-night to enjoy
ourselves in a sociable manner, it is expected that all those that can
sing a song will do so, and those that can recite will do the same, and
as my friend here, the great Poet, McGonagall, can recite, I request
him to open the concert by reciting his own poem,'Bruce at
Bannockburn.'"

I leapt to my feet and said, " Mr Chairman, ladies and gentlemen,— I
refuse to submit to such a request, because I believe in God, and He
has told us to remember the sabbath day to keep it holy, and I
consider it is an act of desecration to hold a concert on the Sabbath.
Therefore, I refuse to recite or sing."

"Oh, but." the Chairman said. "it is all right here in New York. quite
common here."

Then there chanced to be a Jew in the company, and he said to me,
"What you know about God? Did ever He pay your rint?" And I
said, "Perhaps He did. If He didn't come down from Heaven and
pay it Himself, He put it in the minds of some other persons to do it

for Him." Then the Jew said, "You'll petter go home again to Scotland. That won't do here." Then the lady of the house said— "If ya dinna recite to obleege the company ye'll juist need tae gang oot. Ye ought to be ashamed o' yersel, for look how ya have affronted me before my neighbours."

Then I said— "But I haven't affronted God." Then the Jew said— "What you know about God? Did you ever see Him?" " Not in this company at least," I replied. And then I arose and left the company, considering it to be very bad, and retired to my bed for the night, thinking before I fell asleep that I was in dangerous company, because, from my own experience, the people in New York in general have little or no respect for the Sabbath. The theatres are open, also the music halls, and all of them are well patronised. My dear readers, I will now insert in this autobiography of mine a poem, "Jottings of New York," which will give you a little information regarding the ongoings of the people, which runs as follows:—

DESCRIPTIVE POEM — JOTTINGS OF NEW YORK

Oh, mighty city of New York, you are wonderful to behold—
Your buildings are magnificent— the truth be it told—
They were the only thing that seemed to arrest my eye,
Because many of them are thirteen storeys high;
And as for Central Park, it is lovely to be seen—
Especially in the summer season when its shrubberies are green
And the Burns Statue is there to be seen,
Surrounded by trees on the beautiful sward so green;
Also Shakespeare and the immortal Sir Walter Scott,
Which by Scotchmen and Englishmen will never be forgot.

There are people on the Sabbath day in thousands resort—
All lov'd, in conversation, and eager for sport;
And some of them viewing the wild beasts there,
While the joyous shouts of children does rend the air—
And also beautiful black swans, I do declare.

24

And there's beautiful boats to be seen there,
And joyous shouts of children does rend the air,
While the boats sail along with them o'er Lohengrin Lake,
And fare is 5 cents for children, and adults ten is all they take.

And there's also summer-house shades, and merry-go-rounds
And with the merry laughter of the children the Park resounds,
During the live-long Sabbath day
Enjoying themselves at the merry-go-round play.

Then there's the elevated railroads about five storeys high,
Which the inhabitants can hear night and day passing by;
Of, such a mass of people there daily do throng—
No less than five 100,000 daily pass along;
And all along the city you can get for five cents—
And, believe me, among the passengers there's few discontent.

And the top of the houses are mostly all flat,
And in the warm weather the people gather to chat;
Besides, on the housetops they dry their clothes;
And, also, many people all night on the housetops repose.

And numerous ships end steamboats are there to be seen,
Sailing along the East River water, which is very green—
Which is certainly a most beautiful sight
To see them sailing o'er the smooth water day and night.

And as for Brooklyn Bridge, it's a very great height,
And fills the stranger's heart with wonder at first sight;
And with all its loftiness I venture to say
It cannot surpass the new railway bridge of the Silvery Tay.

And there's also ten thousand rumsellers there—
Oh, wonderful to think of, I do declare!
To accommodate the people of New York therein,
And to encourage them to commit all sorts of sin

And on the Sabbath day ye will see many a man
Going for beer with a big tin can,
And seems proud to be seen carrying home the beer
To treat his neighbours and his family dear.

Then at night numbers of the people dance and sing,
Making the walls of their houses to ring
With their songs and dancing on Sabbath night,
Which I witnessed with disgust, and fled from the sight.

And with regard to New York and the sights I did see—
Believe me, I never saw such sights in Dundee;
And the morning I sailed from the city of New York
My heart it felt as light as a cork.

Well, my dear readers, to resume my autobiography, I've told ye I sent a letter to Mr Alexander C. Lamb in Dundee requesting him to fetch me to Dundee as he had promised, and when about three weeks had expired I called at the Anchor Line Steam Shipping Company's office on a Monday morning, I remember, to see if a letter had come from Dundee. Well, when I asked Mr Stewart if there was any news from Dundee, he said, "Yes," smiling at me, and, continuing— "Yes, I received a cablegram from Dundee on Saturday night telling me to give you a passage home again— a second class cabin, not the steerage this time." And he asked me how much money I would require, and I told him about three pounds. "But," he said, "I've been told to give you six," and when he told me so I felt overjoyed, and thanked him and my dear friend, Mr Alexander C. Lamb. Then he asked me if I would take British money or American, and I said I would take American one half and British the other, and along with it he gave me a certificate for my passage on board the "Circassia," which would sail from New York harbour in about a fortnight or so, telling me to be sure and not forget the time the steamer would leave New York for Glasgow, and bidding me to be watchful regarding my money, for there were many bad characters in New York.

Well, my dear friends, I bade him good-bye, telling him I would take his good advice, and, if alive and well, I would be on the lookout for the steamer that was to take me to Bonnie Scotland, and left him with my heart full of glee.

Well, my dear friends, at last the longed-for day arrived that I was to leave New York, and everything I required being ready, I bade farewell to my old Dundee friend and his mistress, and made my way down to the jetty or harbour of New York, where the beautiful steamer "Circassia" lay that I was to embark in, which would carry me safe to Glasgow and the rest of the passengers, God willing. And when I arrived at the jetty there were a great number of intending passengers gathered ready to go on board, and there was a great deal of hand-shaking amongst them, bidding each other good-bye. Some of them were crying bitterly, noticed, end others were seemingly quite happy. Such is life.

> Some do weep, and some feel gay,
> Thus runs the world away.

Well, when the hand-shakings were over, the intending passengers went on board, and I amongst the rest. The first thing that arrested my attention was the skirling of the pibroch, playing "

WILL YE NO COME BACK AGAIN?"

and other old familiar Scottish airs, and the babbling of voices, mingling together with rather discordant music ringing in my ears. The sails were hoisted, and steam got up, and the anchor was weighed, and the bell was rung. Then the vessel steamed out of New York Harbour, bound for Glasgow. The stout vessel sailed o'er the mighty deep, and the passengers felt delighted, especially when an iceberg was sighted. I remember I saw two large ones while going to America. Now, on the return voyage one has been sighted, and a very big one, about ten feet high, which in the distance has a very ghostly appearance, standing there so white, which seemed most fearful to the passengers' sight. And some of the passengers were afraid that it might come towards the vessel, but it remained immovable, which the passengers and captain were very thankful for. Well, on sped the vessel for a week without anything dangerous happening until the sea began all of a sudden to swell, and the waves rose up like mountains high; then the vessel began to roll from side to side in the trough of the sea, and the women began to scream and the children also. The big waves swept o'er her deck, so much so that the hatches had to be nailed down, and we all expected to be drowned in that mighty ocean of waters. Some parts, the steward told me, were five miles deep. When he told me so I said to him, "Is that a fact?" and he said it was really true. And I said to him how wonderful it was and how beautiful and dark blue the sea was, and how I had often heard of

THE DARK BLUE SEA

but now I was sailing o'er it at last. The vessel all at once gave a lurch and slackened her speed, and the cause thereof was owing to the piston of one of the engines breaking in the centre, which rendered it unworkable, and it couldn't be repaired until the vessel arrived in Glasgow. By that break in the engine we were delayed three days longer at sea, and, strange to say as I remarked to some of the passengers, "Isn't it wonderful to think that the sea calmed down all at once as soon as the piston broke?" And some said it was and others said it wasn't, and I said in my opinion it was God that calmed the sea— that it was a Providential interference, for, if the sea hadn't calmed down, the vessel would have been useless amongst the big waves owing to the engine giving way, and would have sunk with us all to the bottom of the briny deep, and not one of us would have been saved. Well, my friends, after that I was looked upon as a prophet and a God-fearing man, and very much respected by the passengers and the chief steward. So on the next evening there was to he a concert held amongst the passengers, and they all felt happy that they were spared from a watery grave, and many of them thanked God for saving them from being drowned. So the next day the sea was as calm as a mirror, and the vessel skimmed o'er the smooth waters like a bird on the wing, and the passengers felt so delighted that some of them began to sing. When evening set in, and the passengers had got their tea, arrangements were made to hold the concert in the cabin saloon, as formerly, and, of course, I was invited, as before, to give my services. This is generally expected on board of all emigrant vessels. Any one known to be a singer or a reciter will join in the entertainment for the evening, because emigrants either going or returning from a foreign country are all like one family. There seems to be a brotherly and a sisterly feeling amongst them, more so at sea than on land. No doubt the reason is that they are more afraid of losing their lives at sea than on land.

A CONCERT AT SEA

When it drew nigh to eight o'clock all those who intended to be present at the concert began to assemble in the cabin saloon, and by eight o'clock the saloon was well filled with a very select gathering of passengers. Of course, amongst them was the chief steward and myself as formerly. Of course he was elected as chairman, and as formerly he announced that all collections of money on board at concerts went for the benefit of the Lifeboat Fund. Now there was amongst the passengers an actor, who had been to New York in expectation of getting engagements there, and had failed, and was well known to the chief steward, and had consented to give a recital along with a lady from the play of "The Lady of Lyons." She was to read her part from the book, and he was to recite his part from memory, he taking the part of Claude Mellnotte, and she "the Lady of Lyons." So such being the case the audience thought they were going to get a treat, so the chairman announced them as first on the programme to give a recital, which was received with applause when announced. But that was all the applause they received during their recital, for she stammered all along in the reading of her part, and as for the actor he wasn't much better. All the difference was he remembered his part, but his voice was bad. Then when they had finished their recital I was requested to give a recital, and I recited Othello's Apology, which was received with great applause. Then I was encored, and for an encore I sang "The Rattling Boy from Dublin," and received thunders of applause. When I had finished several of the passengers shook hands with me warmly, telling me I had done well. Then other songs followed from ladies and gentlemen. And the chairman sang a song, and we all felt quite jolly, and free from melancholy, while the vessel sped on steadily as a rock. By this time it was near ten o'clock, and us it was near time to finish up with the concert, I was requested by the chairman to give another recital, which would conclude the evening's entertainment. So I consented, and recited "The Battle of Tel-el-Kebir," and received the general applause of the audience. This finished the evening's entertainment. Then there was shaking of hands amongst the passengers, and high compliments were paid to those that joined in the concert, myself included. So we all retired to rest, highly pleased with the evening's entertainment, and I slept fairly well that night. In the morning I was awakened from my sleep by someone knocking at the door of my berth, gently, and I asked who was there. A voice replied, "A friend." I arose at once to see who had knocked, and there was one of the gentlemen who had heard me recite at the concert, and he asked me if I was open to receive from him a few shillings as

A TOKEN OF REWARD

and his appreciation of my abilities as a reciter, telling me he considered it a great shame for passengers to allow me to give them so much for nothing. so I thanked him for his kindness, and he said— "Don't mention it," and bade me good morning, saying he was going to have breakfast, and that he would see me again. So in a short time the bell rang for breakfast, and I was served, as well as others, with a small loaf of bread and butter and a large tin of hot coffee, which in general is the morning fare— quite enough, in my opinion, for any ordinary man.Well, my friends, I have nothing more of any importance to relate concerning my return from New York, any more than that we arrived safe and well at Glasgow, after being fourteen days at sea on the home-coming voyage. The next morning I took an early train bound for Dundee, and arrived there shortly after one o'clock noon. When I arrived at home my family were very glad to see me; and also some of my old friends; and as I had written a diary regarding my trip to New York I sold it to a newspaper reporter, who gave me 7s. 6d. for it.

FAREWELL TO DUNDEE

Well, my dear friends, the next event in my life that I am going to relate is regarding me and my Mistress McGonagall leaving Dundee in the year 1894, resolving to return no more owing to the harsh treatment I had received in the city as is well known for a truth without me recording it. Well, I went to the Fair City of Perth, one of the finest upon the earth, intending to remain there altogether. So I secured a small garret in the South Street, and me and my mistress lived there for eight months, and the inhabitants were very kind to us in many respects. But I remember receiving a letter from an Inverness gentleman requesting me to come through on the 16th October and give him and his friends an entertainment, and that all arrangements had been made with the directors of the Inverness Railway Company, and that I had only to show the letter. I went down to the Railway Station and showed the official the letter from Inverness inviting me through, and when they read it they said it was all right. They had received a telegram regarding it, and they told me to come down in the morning a little before ten o'clock, so as I could leave Perth with the ten o'clock train, and they would give me a certificate that would make me all right for the return journey to Perth. So I thanked them, telling them I would be down in the morning, God willing, in good time. When I went home I told my wife that I had made all right for my railway trip to Inverness, and she was glad to hear that it was all right. When I had got my supper I went to bed, but I didn't sleep well, for I was thinking too much about venturing so far away entirely amongst strangers, but as I had been assured of

A HEARTY HIGHLAND WELCOME

I considered I was safe in making the venture. So I screwed up my courage and all danger regarding my trip to Inverness vanished from my mind. In the morning I arose and donned my clothes, and partook of a hearty meal along with my good lady, and then made myself ready for going to Inverness. When ready I bade my mistress good-bye, and away I went to the railway station and saw the officials. When the train for Inverness was nearly ready to start they showed me into one of the carriages, and bade me good-bye.

The train steamed off with its long white curling cloud of steam which was most beautiful to be seen. The train passed rocky mountains and woodland scenery, and lochs and rivers, and clear crystal fountains gushing from the mountains, and the bleak, heathery hills made the scenery very romantic to the appearance I remember. But it was only a bird's eye view I had, the train passed on so quickly, but in the summer season I thought it would be delightful to be roaming at ease, and to be viewing the mountain scenery and the beautiful villas by the way near to the riverside, surrounded by trees and shrubberies. As for the angler, he could have excellent sport fishing in the lochs and the river in that Highland region near to Dalwhinnie and other beautiful places I noticed by the way. And while thinking so in my mind I was astonished to think that the train had arrived, before I knew, and there I was met at the station by the gentleman who had written to me. He asked me if I was the Poet McGonagall, and I add I was, and he grasped me by the hand kindly, and told me to follow him. I did so without fear, and he took me to a hotel. And as we entered it we were met by the landlord, to whom I was introduced. And the proprietor told me there and then not to be ashamed to ask for anything I liked that was in the house, and I would get it, because the gentleman that had fetched me through from Perth had told him so, and with that my friend left me to my own meditations. Then I told the hotel proprietor I would have for dinner some coffee, bread, and a beefsteak, so in a very short space of time my dinner was ready and served out to me by a servant girl, and I did ample justice to it because I felt hungry. By this time it was about five o'clock in the afternoon, so I went out to have a walk and view the beautiful scenery along the riverside, and after I did so it was within an hour for me to entertain the gentleman who had brought me from Perth, so I had some tea made ready, and ate heartily, and when finished my friend came in and asked me if I had been enjoying myself, and I told him I had. Then he said the gentlemen I was to entertain would soon drop in. So they began to drop in by twos and threes until the room was well filled. The large table in the room was well spread with costly viands. When we had all partaken of the good spread on the table a chairman was elected, a gentlemen of the name of Mr Gossip, and a very nice gentlemen he was. He began by saying— " Gentlemen! I feel proud to-night to be elected at this meeting of friends and acquaintances to hear the great poet, Mr McGonagall, displaying his poetic abilities from his own works and from other poets also, and I request, gentlemen, that we will give him a patient hearing, and I am sure if ye do ye will get a poetic treat, for his name is a household word at the present day. Therefore, gentlemen, with these few remarks I will call upon our distinguished guest, Mr McGonagall, to favour the company with a recital of his famous poem, 'Bannockburn.'"

I arose and said— "Gentlemen, I feel proud to-night to be amongst such a select company of gentlemen, and as far as my abilities will permit me I'll endeavour to please ye, and by your kind permission I will now begin to recite my Bannockburn poem."

Before I was halfway through, the cheering from the company was really deafening to my ears, so much so that I had to halt until the cheering subsided, and when I finished the company shook hands with me all round. After I sat down one of the gentlemen said he would sing a song on my behalf while I was resting, but he said he would need to get a glass of wine first. So when he got the glass of wine and drank to my health he began to sing that song of Burns', "Gae bring tae me a pint of wine." I can assure ye, my readers, he sang the song very well, and with so much vehemence that when he had finished

HE WAS FAIRLY EXHAUSTED

and all for my sake. And when done his head fell upon his shoulder, and he seemed to be in the arms of Morpheus. Then other gentlemen sang songs, and the night passed by pleasantly, and all went well. Then the chairman said— "Gentlemen, as the night is far advanced I will now call upon our guest of the evening, Mr McGonagall, to give us a song— 'The Rattling Boy from Dublin,' of which he is the author." Then I said— "Mr chairman and gentlemen, I am quite willing to do so, owing to the kind treatment I have met with, and the hearty Highland welcome ye have bestowed upon me, which I will not forget in a hurry. So I will begin to sing my song." Before I was halfway through, the gentleman who had fallen asleep in the chair awoke, and leapt on to the floor, and began to dance, until the chairman had to stop him from dancing, and when order was restored I went on with my song without any further interruption. And when I finished my song I recited "The Battle of Tel-el-Kebir," also a scene from Macbeth, which seemed to please the company very well. That was owing, I think, to Macbeth living in Inverness at one time.

Well, my dear friends, that concluded the evening's entertainment. Then the gentleman who had sent me the letter to come through to Inverness to give his friends an entertainment arose and said— "Mr chairman and friends,— It now falls to my lot to present to the great poet, McGonagall, this purse of silver, of which it is the desire of my friends and myself never to make known the contents." So saying, he handed me the purse and its contents, which I thanked him for and the company, telling them that I would never forget their kindness, and that in all my travels I had never met with such good treatment. Then the gentlemen all round shook hands with me, declaring they were well pleased with the entertainment I had given them. Wishing me good night and a sound sleep, they left me to my own meditations; but my friend, before leaving me, conducted me to my bed in the hotel, and wishing me good-night, he said he would see me in the morning, and see me off in the train for Perth. So I went to bed, quite delighted with the treatment I had received from the gentlemen I had entertained in Inverness, and in the morning I was up with the lark, and had a good breakfast, and put a good luncheon piece in my pocket to eat by the way returning to Perth. My friend called on me in the morning, and accompanied me to the Railway Station, and saw me off by the ten o'clock train for Perth, and I arrived safe in Perth about half-past four o'clock on the afternoon of the 17th day of October, 1894.

Two days after my arrival from Inverness I composed a poem in praise of the Heather Blend Club banquet at Inverness, which is as follows:-

'Twas on the 16th of October, in the year 1894,
I was invited to Inverness, not far from the sea shore,
To partake of a banquet prepared by the Heather Blend Club,
Gentlemen who honoured me without any hubbub.

The banquet was held in the Gellion Hotel,
And the landlord, Mr Macpherson, treated me right well;
Also the servant maids were very kind to me,
Especially the girl that polished my boots, most beautiful to see.

The banquet consisted of roast beef, potatoes, and red wine;
Also hare soup and sherry and grapes most fine,
And baked pudding and apples lovely to be seen;
Also rich sweet milk and delicious cream.

Mr Gossip, a noble Highlander, acted as chairman,
And when the banquet was finished the fun began;
And I was requested to give a poetic entertainment,
Which I gave, and which pleased them to their hearts' content.

And for my entertainment they did me well reward
By titling me there the Heather Blend Club bard;
Likewise I received an illuminated address,
Also a purse of silver, I honestly confess.

Oh, magnificent city of Inverness,
And your beautiful river, I must confess,

With its lovely scenery on each side,
Would be good for one's health there to reside.

There the blackbird and mavis together doth sing,
Making the woodlands with their echoes to ring
During the months of July, May, and June,
When the trees and the shrubberies are in full bloom.

And to see the River Ness rolling smoothly along,
Together with the blackbird's musical song,
While the sun shines bright in the month of May,
Will help to drive dull care away.

And Macbeth's Castle is grand to be seen,
Situated on Castle Hill, which is beautiful and green.
'Twas there Macbeth lived in days of old,
And a very great tyrant he was be it told.

I wish the members of the Heather Blend Club every success,
Hoping God will prosper them and bless;
Long may Dame Fortune smile upon them,
For all of them I've met are kind gentlemen.

And in praise of them I must say
I never received better treatment in my day,
Than I received from my admirers in Bonnie Inverness.
This, upon my soul and conscience, I do confess.

My dear readers, I must now give you a brief account of my trip to the mighty city of London. If I can remember, it might be either 19 or 20 years ago, and in the merry month of June, when trees and flowers were in full bloom, and owing to my poverty I couldn't have gone to London, only that I recieved a letter — a forged one — supposed to be written by Dion Boucicault, the Irish dramatist, inviting me down to Stratton's Restaurant at twelve o'clock noon to have lunch with him, as he intended to engage me for a provincial tour to give entertainments in the provincial towns throughout Britain, and he would give me a big salary. Well, my dear friends, of course I felt delighted when I read the letter, so I went to Stratton's Restaurant just as the town clock struck twelve. I was received very kindly, and shown upstairs to a little room. I think it was the smoking room, and I knocked at the door, and it was answered by one of the gentlemen. Of course I knew him, and he introduced me to the gentleman who was impersonating the character of Dion Boucicault, and he asked me how I was, and I told him I was very well, hoping to find him the same. Then he told me he had heard so much about my histrionic abilities that he would engage me and give me a salary of £20 weekly, food included, and the other gentlemen present said it was little enough for a man of my abilities; but all the while I know he was an impostor. Then he requested me to recite my famous poem, "Bruce at Bannockburn," and of course I did so, and when finished he declared if I would recite that before a Scottish audience in London it would pull down the house. Then he told one of the gentlemen to fetch in some refreshment for Mr McGonagall, for he was more then delighted with my Bannockburn recital. Then a gentleman waiter came in with a little refreshment on a tea tray, simply

A penny sandwich and a tumbler of beer,
Thinking it would my spirits cheer.

And I remember I looked at it with a scornful eye before I took it, and I laid it down on a little round table beside me and screwed my courage to the sticking place, and stared the impostor Boucicault in the face, and he felt rather uneasy, like he guessed I knew he wasn't the original Boucicault, so he arose from his seat and made a quick retreat, and before leaving he bade me good-bye, telling me he would see me again. Then I kept silent, and I stared the rest of my pretended friends out of countenance until they couldn't endure the penetrating glance of my poetic eye, so they arose and left me alone in my glory. Then I partook of the grand penny luncheon I had received for my recital of "Bannockburn," and with indignation my heart did burn.

I went direct to the Theatre Royal, and inquired for Mr Hodge, the manager, and I saw him and I showed him the letter I had received from Dion Boucicault, as I didn't believe it was from him, and when he looked at it he said it wasn't his handwriting, and how I had met with a great disappointment no doubt, and asked me if I would allow him to make an extract from the letter and he would send it to Boucicault, so I said I would; so he made an extract, telling me he mentioned my poor circumstances in it, and he had no doubt but Mr Boucicault would do something for me by way of solatium for my wounded feelings and for using his name in vain. He told me to come down to the theatre inside of three days, and he would have a letter from Boucicault by that time, he expected, so I thanked him for his kindness, and came away with my spirits light and gay.

Well, I waited patiently till the three days were expired, then called at the Theatre Royal and saw Mr Hodge, the manager, and he received me very kindly, telling me he had received a letter from Mr Boucicault with a £5 cheque in it on the Bank of Scotland, so he handed me five sovereigns in gold along with Boucicault's letter. I thanked him and came away, and in the letter Boucicault felt for me very much, saying practical jokers were practical fools, which in my opinion is really true. So, my dear readers, it was through me getting the £5 from Boucicault that I resolved to take a

TRIP TO LONDON.

A steerage return passage at that time was £1, so I purchased a ticket and made up my mind to go. I remember it was in the month of June, when trees and flowers were in full bloom, and on a Wednesday afternoon I embarked on board the steamer "London," and there were a few of my friends waiting patiently at the dockyard to see me off to London and wish me success in my perilous enterprise, and to give me a hearty cheer my spirits for to cheer, and a merry shake of hands all round, which made the dockyard loudly resound. Then when the handshakings were o'er the steam whistle began to roar. Then the engine started, and the steamer left the shore, while she sailed smoothly o'er the waters of the Tay, and the passengers' hearts felt light and gay. There weren't many passengers, I remember, but seemingly they all felt merry as the steamer drew near to Broughty Ferry, because the scenery in that direction is very fascinating to be seen, the seascape so lovely and green. When the steamer had passed by Broughty Ferry a few miles I remember the passengers began to get weary, and we were all sitting on the deck, and some of them proposed that they should have a song, so a lady sang a song, but I don't remember the name of it; it's so long ago, but it's of no great consequence. When they had all sung I was requested to give a recital, and I gave them the "Battle of Tel-el-Kebir," which was well received, and I got an encore, and I gave them the "Rattling Boy from Dublin Town," and for which I received a small donation, and that finished the entertainment for the night. Then the steerage passengers bade me good-night and retired to their berths for the night, and me along with the rest. Well, the steamer sailed smoothly along during the night, and nothing happened that would the most timid heart affright, and the passengers slept well, including myself, owing to the smooth sailing of the good ship.

All went smoothly as a marriage bell until the good steamer landed us safe at the wharf, London, in the River Thames. Then there was shaking of hands and bidding each other good-bye, and each one took their own way, some on holiday, others on the look-out for work; such was the case with me. Well, as soon as I got ashore I held on by the Fish Market, and as I drew near very discordant sounds broke upon my ear. The babbling of the fishmongers was disagreeable to hear; and I had my properties with me in a black bag, and as I was passing along where there were about thirty men lounging near to the market-place they cried after me, " Hi! hi!

Scottie, I'll carry your bag," but I paid no heed to them, because I would never have seen it if I had allowed anyone of them to have carried the bag. However, I made my way to Fetter Lane, Fleet Street, and secured my lodgings for a week in the White Horse Inn, Fetter Lane, at 4d. per night, so for the time being I was all right.

I PAID THE LANDLORD IN ADVANCE

for my lodging, and had some supper, and then I gave him my bag to lock up; then my mind felt quite at ease. Then I went out to have a walk, and resolved to call at the Lyceum Theatre and see — now Sir — Henry Irving. He wasn't Sir Henry then, my friends. Well, I made straight for the theatre and saw the janitor at the stage entrance, and I asked him if I could see Mr Irving, and he said snappishly I could not, and that Mr Irving wouldn't speak to the likes of me. Well, of course, I felt indignant, and I told him I considered myself to be as great a man as he is, and came away without delay; but he will speak to me now, my friends, and has done so in Edinburgh. Well, after I had come home to my lodgings from the theatre I made my supper quickly, and relished it with a good appetite. I requested the landlord to show me to bed, and he did so cheerfully, and wished me good-night and sweet repose. Each lodger had an enclosed apartment to himself of wood and a door, which he can lock if he likes to do so. However, I went to bed and slept soundly during the night, and arose in the morning, when the sun was shining bright. Then I donned my clothes, and made my breakfast, and took it with great gusto; then, when finished, I went out and wended my way towards London Bridge, and, oh! such a busy throng of cabs and 'buses rapidly whirling along. After viewing it, I returned to my lodging quite delighted with the sight I had seen, and then I prepared my dinner a few hours afterwards, and ate heartily. Then I went to some of the Music Halls looking for engagements, but, unfortunately, I didn't succeed. Owing to the disappointments I met with, I resolved to return home to Dundee as soon as possible. Well, when Sabbath came round, I went to the Tabernacle to hear Mr Spurgeon preach, and I most solemnly declare he is the greatest preacher I've ever heard, with the exception of Gilfillan.

However, as I resolved to return home to Dundee, I waited for the day Saturday to come. That was the day the steamer "London" would leave London for Dundee, and when Saturday came I left my lodgings in Fetter Lane, longing, of course, for to get hame, and embarked on board, with my heart light, and longing to see the Silvery Tay. So the stout steamer from the Thames sailed away, and arrived on Wednesday in the Silvery Tay, and the passengers' hearts were full of glee when they were landed safely in Dundee once again. I was glad to see it, especially my family. In conclusion, I will insert my poem,

"JOTTINGS OF LONDON"

As I stood upon London Bridge,
And viewed the mighty throng
Of thousands of people in cabs and 'buses
Rapidly whirling along,
And driving to and fro,
Up one street and down another
As quick as they could go.

Then I was struck with the discordant sound
Of human voices there,
Which seemed to me like wild geese
Cackling in the air.

And as for the River Thames —
It is a most wonderful sight;
To see the steamers and barges
Sailing up and down upon it
From early morn till night.

And as for the Tower of London —
It is most gloomy to behold,
And within it lies the Crown of England
Begemmed with precious stones and gold.

Kingly Henry the Sixth was murdered there
By the Duke of Gloster,
And when he killed him with his sword
He called him an impostor.

St. Paul's Cathedral is the finest building
That ever I did see;
There's nothing can surpass it
In the town of Dundee,
For it is most magnificent to behold
With its beautiful dome and lofty spire glittering like gold.

And as for Nelson's Monument
That stands in Trafalgar Square—
It is a most stately statue
I most solemnly declare,
And towering very high,
Which arrests strangers' attention
When they are passing by.
And there's two beautiful water fountains
Spouting up very high,
Where the weary travellers can have a drink
When they feel dry

Then at the foot of Nelson's Monument
There's three figures of bronze lions in grand array,
Which ought to drive dull care away
As the stranger gazes thereon,
Unless he is very woebegone.

Then as for Mr Spurgeon,
He is a divine surgeon,
Which no one can gainsay.
I went to hear him preach on the Sabbath day.
Which made my heart feel light and gay
For to hear him preach and pray.

And the Tabernacle was crowded from ceiling to floor,
And many people were standing outside the door.
He is an eloquent preacher, I solemnly declare,
And I was struck with admiration as I on him did stare;
For he is the only individual I heard
Speaking proper English during my stay there.

Then as for Petticoat Lane, I venture to say
It's a most wonderful place to see on the Sabbath day;
For wearing apparel of every kind
Can be bought to suit the young and the old
For the ready money— silver, copper, or gold.

My Dear Readers—I must now tell ye my reason for leaving the Fair City of Perth. It was because I found it to be too small for me making a living in. I must allow, the inhabitants were very kind to me during my stay amongst them. And while living there I received a letter, and when I opened it I was struck with amazement when I found a silver elephant enclosed, and I looked at it in amazement, and said— "I'll now have a look at this big letter enclosed. I was astonished to see that King Theebaw, of Burmah and the Andaman Islands, had conferred upon me the honorary title of Sir Wm. Topaz McGonagall, Knight of The White Elephant, Burmah, and for the benefit of my readers and the public, I consider I am justified in recording it in my autobiography, which runs as follows:—

> *Court of King Theebaw,*
> *Andaman Islands,*
> *Dec. 2, 1894.*

Dear and Most Highly Honoured Sir,—Having the great honour to belong to the same holy fraternity of poets as yourself, I have been requested by our fellow-country-men at present serving our Queen and country in Her Majesty's great Indian Empire to send you the following address, and at the same time to inform you that you were lately appointed a Grand Knight of the Holy Order of the White Elephant, by his Royal Highness upon representation being made to him by your fellow-countrymen out here

King Theebaw, who is just now holding his Court in the Andeman Islands, expressed himself as being only too pleased to confer the highest honour possible upon merit, wheresoever found, if that merit were judged worthy by his Grand Topaz General. As the latter gentleman has long been impressed by the injustice with which you have been treated by Lord Rosebery in his position as chief adviser of Her Majesty, and since your great modesty upon several occasions has been noticed by His Royal Highness the King of Burmah, it gives him great pleasure to assure Theebaw, the King, that none more worthy of this high honour has ever lived in the East, whereat His Royal Highness called his Court together, and with much eclat and esteem caused it to be proclaimed throughout his present palace and kingdom that you were to be known henceforth as Topaz McGonagall, G.K.H.O.W.E.B.

Should you ever visit the Andaman Islands it will be his great pleasure to be presented to you, and to do all honour to you, according to the very ancient custom with which members of our mutual illustrious Order have always been treated by his ancestors.

That you will consent to accept the high honour now offered to you is the wish nearest the hearts of your countrymen in the East; that you may be long spared to enrich British literature by your grand and thrilling works is their most sincere prayer.

His Majesty also expressed it as his opinion, and the opinion of his grandfathers as far back as the flood, that such talented works as those of their holy fraternity of poets were, had always been, and for ever would be, above all earthly praise, their value being inestimable. Be further stated that he failed to conceive how Rosebery could have been so blind as not to have offered to such a man as yourself the paltry and mean stipend attached to the position of Poet Laureate of Great Britain and Ireland. It is indescribable to him that any man of ordinary rummel gumption could possibly offer remuneration to such a gift of the Gods as yours.

Should you see fit to do the ancient Kingdom of Burmah the honour of accepting the Ribbon of its highest Order, and will kindly pay its capital a visit at your earliest convenience, it is the King's order that you be received with all the ceremony due to the greatest ornament now living of the Holy Order of the White Elephant. You are to be immediately installed in the holy chair of the Knights of the above Order upon arrival, from which it is the custom of the holy fraternity to address the whole Eastern world.

King Theebaw will not injure your sensitive feelings by offering you any filthy lucre as payment for what you may compose in his honour after receiving the insignia of the Holy Order. He also states it will be his duty to see that your name is duly reverenced throughout the Kingdom.

I have the honour to be, most noble and illustrious sir, your most humble brother in the fraternity of poets.

> *(Per) C.MACDONALD, K.O.W.E.B,*
> *Poet Laureate of Burmah.*

By order of His Royal Highness the King.
Topaz General.
Topaz Minister.
Secretary of State.
Holder of Seals.
Registrar-General.
Staff-Bearer.
Secretary of Letters Patent.
Keeper of the White Elephant.

My dear readers, this letter regarding my knighthood is a correct copy from the original as near as I can write it, with the exception of the Indian language therein, which means the names of the gentlemen that signed the Royal patent letter regarding my knighthood. That is all that is wanting, which I cannot write or imitate. Nor can I imitate the four red seals that are affixed to the Royal document. The insignia of the knighthood is a silver elephant attached to a green silk ribbon. This, my dear readers, is the full particulars regarding my Indian knighthood, and, my dear friends and well-wishers, I must conclude this autobiography of mine by truthfully recording herein that since I came to beautiful Edinburgh, and that is more than six years now past, I have received the very best of treatment, and during my stay in Edinburgh I have given many entertainments from my own poetic works, also from Shakespeare.

I may say I have been highly appreciated by select audiences, and for their appreciation of my abilities I return them my sincere thanks for being so kind as to give me their support since I came to Edinburgh.— My dear friends, I am, yours faithfully,

Sir Wm. Topaz McGonagall,
Poet and Knight of the White Elephant, Burmah.

Lightning Source UK Ltd.
Milton Keynes UK
UKOW050824210911

179040UK00002B/92/P